ISBN 0-439-29517-3

Copyright © 2000 by Jez Alborough. All rights reserved.
Published by Scholastic Inc., 555 Broadway, New York, NY 10012,
by arrangement with Candlewick Press. SCHOLASTIC and associated
logos are trademarks and/or registered trademarks of Scholastic Inc.

12 11 10 9 8   8 9 10 11/0

Printed in the U.S.A.   08

First Scholastic printing, October 2001

This book was hand lettered by the author-illustrator.
The illustrations were done in marker pen.

HUG

Jez Alborough

SCHOLASTIC INC.

New York Toronto London Auckland Sydney
Mexico City New Delhi Hong Kong

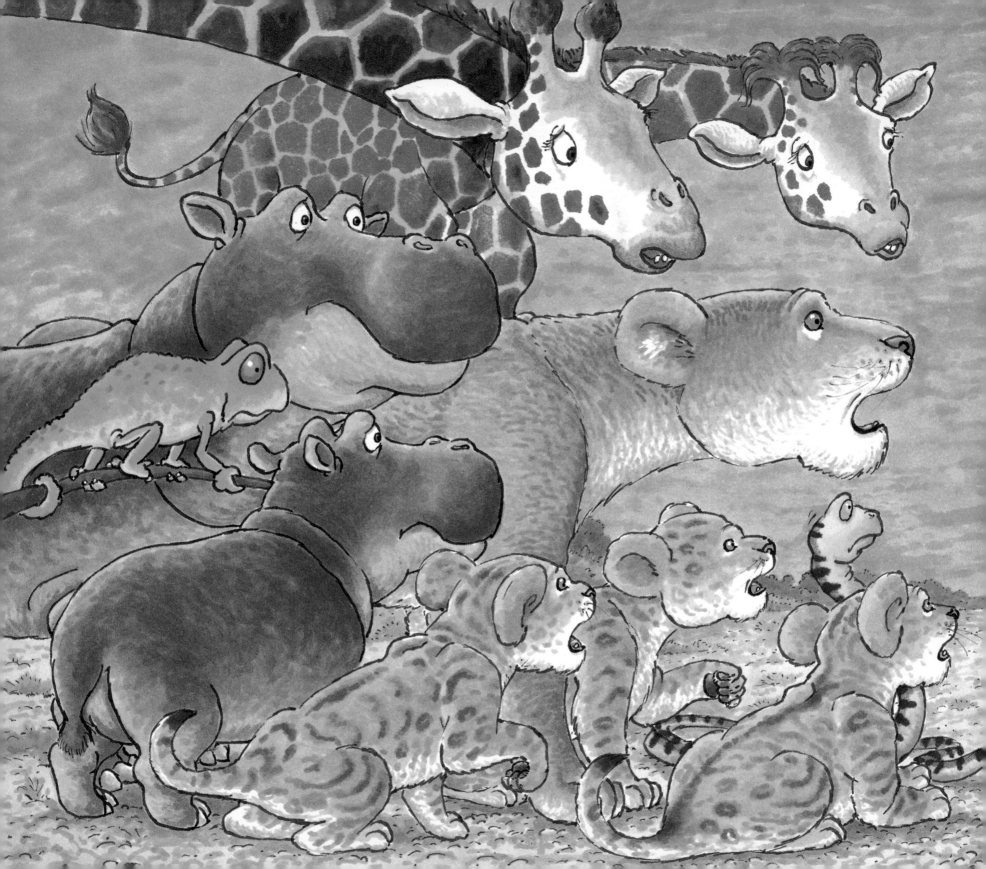

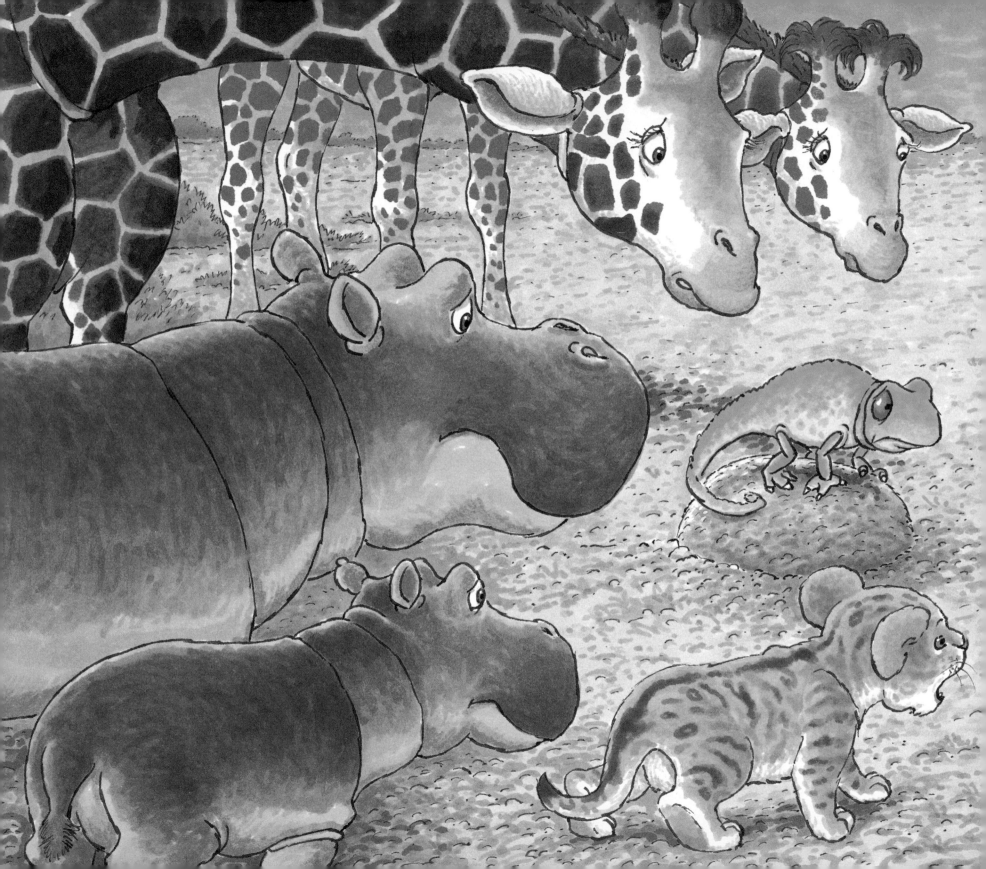